Meet the Lalaloopsy Girls

ISBN 978-0-545-37997-7

12 11 10 9 8 7 6 5 4

12 13 14 15 16 / 0

Designed by Angela Jun and Two Red Shoes Design
Printed in the U.S.A.
First printing, September 2011

40

Lalaloopsy™
Sew Magical! Sew Cute!

Meet the Lalaloopsy Girls

by Samantha Brooke

SCHOLASTIC INC.

New York   Toronto   London   Auckland   Sydney   Mexico City   New Delhi   Hong Kong

Spot Splatter Splash

Bea Spells-a-Lot

Welcome to
Lalaloopsy Land—
a fantastical world full
of silly surprises!

Dot Starlight

Peanut Big

4

Mittens
Fluff 'N' Stuff

Jewel Sparkles

Crumbs
Sugar Cookie

Pillow Featherbed

Park

5

The Lalaloopsy dolls were once rag dolls that magically came to life when their very last stitch was sewn.

Crumbs   Jewel   Dot   Peanut

Each doll has a special personality that comes from the fabrics that were used to make her.

Bea

Mittens

Pillow

Spot

Crumbs Sugar Cookie™

Crumbs was made from a piece of yellow-and-white apron. The baker who once owned this apron spent lots of time in the kitchen cooking up yummy treats.

Once Crumbs' very last stitch was sewn, she sprang to life with a love of everything super sweet. Crumbs often can be found in the kitchen creating new recipes to share with her friends. She and her pet mouse make the perfect team: She bakes the cookies and her mouse eats the crumbs!

Date Last Stitch Was Sewn:
December 4th
(National Cookie Day)
Pet: Mouse
Likes: Bake sales
Dislikes: Burned cookies
Most Likely to Say:
"Life is sweet."

Jewel Sparkles™

Jewel was made from a piece of a princess' polka-dotted dress. The princess who once owned this dress wore it while twirling across the dance floor at many royal balls.

When Jewel's last stitch was sewn, she pirouetted to life! She's very graceful, a little bit bossy, and loves to wear sparkly clothes. When she's not practicing how to curtsy, she can usually be found playing with her Persian cat, a very royal pet indeed!

Date Last Stitch Was Sewn:
March 13th (Jewel Day)
Pet: Persian cat
Likes: anything glittery
Dislikes: Rainy days
Most Likely to Say:
"Isn't this just perfectly perfect?"

Dot Starlight

Dot was made from an astronaut's shiny silver spacesuit. The astronaut who once wore this suit flew high above the Earth in a spaceship and even got to walk on the moon!

When Dot's last stitch was sewn, she rocketed to life! Dot's a dreamer who loves science, and she's always got her head in the clouds. Her copilot on all her high-flying adventures is her lovable pet bird.

Date Last Stitch Was Sewn:
July 20th
(First Man on the Moon)
Pet: Bird
Likes: airplanes
Dislikes: Gravity
Most Likely to Say:
"Twinkle, twinkle, little star . . ."

Peanut Big Top™

Peanut was made from bits of a brightly colored clown costume. The circus clown who once owned this costume loved to juggle and do somersaults on the trampoline.

Once Peanut's last stitch was sewn, she burst to life with a huge smile! Peanut's a silly prankster who loves to make her friends laugh. And what could be a better pet for a circus-loving girl than an elephant?

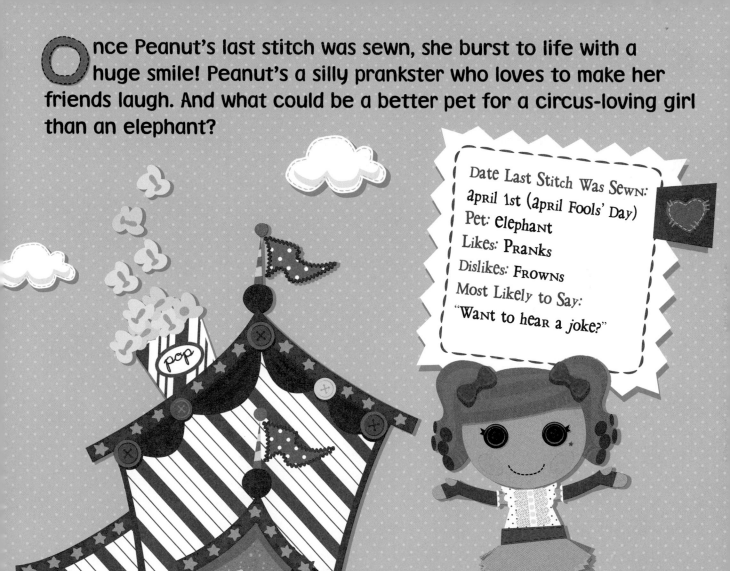

Date Last Stitch Was Sewn:
April 1st (April Fools' Day)
Pet: elephant
Likes: Pranks
Dislikes: Frowns
Most Likely to Say:
"Want to hear a joke?"

Bea Spells-a-Lot

Bea was made from a school girl's uniform. The girl who once wore this uniform never got into trouble—probably because she was so busy reading!

When Bea's last stitch was sewn, she came to life practically singing the alphabet! Bea's a real bookworm and she always follows the rules. At night, she likes to read under the covers with a flashlight while her pet owl hoots at the moon.

Date Last Stitch Was Sewn:
October 16th (Dictionary Day)
Pet: Owl
Likes: Books
Dislikes: Being late
Most Likely to Say:
"Let's go to the library."

Bea was here

ABC 123

stop

Mittens Fluff 'N' Stuff™

Mittens was made from pieces of an Eskimo's blue-and-white scarf. The Eskimo who once owned this scarf was great at building snowmen and used his scarf to keep warm.

Once Mittens' last stitch was sewn, she jumped to life—ready for a snowball fight! She likes hot cocoa, sledding, and snuggling by the fire. Mittens and her cuddly pet polar bear especially love slipping and sliding on the ice.

Date Last Stitch Was Sewn:
December 21st
(First Day of Winter)
Pet: Polar bear
Likes: Making snow angels
Dislikes: Melting icicles
Most Likely to Say:
"Let's build a snowman!"

Pillow Featherbed™

Pillow was made from pieces of a baby's orange-and-white striped blanket. The baby who cuddled with this blankie loved to giggle all day long.

When Pillow's last stitch was sewn, she went right to sleep! Pillow loves hearing bedtime stories, taking afternoon naps, and snacking on milk and cookies. Pillow's pet sheep follows her everywhere she goes and is the perfect snuggling companion!

Date Last Stitch Was Sewn: January 3rd (Festival of Sleep Day)
Pet: Sheep
Likes: Sweet dreams
Dislikes: alarm clocks
Most Likely to Say: "Zzzzzz"

Spot Splatter Splash™

Spot was made from a painter's overalls. The artist who once wore these overalls created dazzling works of art that have been shown in museums around the world.

22

Once Spot's last stitch was sewn, she painted the world around her. Spot is super creative and loves bright colors and big messes. Even her pet zebra has some spots of its own!

Date Last Stitch Was Sewn:
October 25th
(International Artist Day)
Pet: Zebra
Likes: Rainbows
Dislikes: Cleaning up
Most Likely to Say:
"Let's paint a rainbow!"

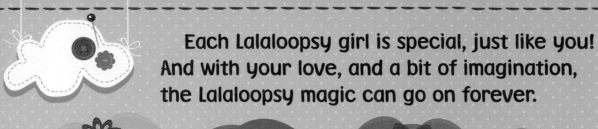

Each Lalaloopsy girl is special, just like you!
And with your love, and a bit of imagination,
the Lalaloopsy magic can go on forever.